# Stranger at the Gates

Written by David Hunt
and illustrated by Alex Brychta

# Chapter 1

The Viran stood quietly, watching. From the ridge where he was, he could see the Viking camp. Smoke from their fires gently rose in the morning air. It all looked so peaceful.

His eyes wandered beyond the camp's jagged wooden walls, over a forest to a muddy field some half-mile away. There, delicate trails of rising smoke marked another camp. The Saxon army camp. His camp.

The Viran's mind drifted back to how it all began. Like an icy wind from the north, the Vikings had swept through the Saxon kingdom. For a time, the Saxon king, Alfred, had been on the run. Alfred's kingdom was in chaos. The Viran smiled when he remembered this. He had joined King Alfred's army for one reason only – he wanted to keep the war against the Vikings going, and ruin any chance of peace.

But now things seemed to be going well for Alfred at last. The Saxons had driven the Vikings back and surrounded their camp. The Vikings were trapped and had little food. They were close to surrendering. The Viran had to keep the battle going – but how?

"Hey!" A voice interrupted the Viran's thoughts. "Wulfgar!" It was Rodor, the son of one of King Alfred's chief men. "Are you going to help me with this or not?"

Rodor was standing by a heap of branches. It was Rodor and Wulfgar's job to stack the branches into a bonfire, called a beacon. If there was any trouble, the beacon could be lit and the fire would be seen for miles. It would be a signal to tell the Saxons to fight.

"Whatever you say, young sire!" mumbled Wulfgar. They stacked the branches in silence, till Rodor suddenly spoke.

"I don't see the point of this beacon," he said. "I mean, the Vikings are hungry and weak, so they won't fight. And as for King Alfred, he wants to make peace with the Vikings. We won't be lighting this, I can tell you."

"Hmmm," rasped Wulfgar, but he said nothing more. His Viran mind was working fast.

Rodor threw the last of the branches on the stack. “Done,” he said. “Let’s go.”

Wulfgar watched Rodor proudly straighten the gold brooch on his tunic. The brooch was from King Alfred. It meant Rodor was important.

All at once, Wulfgar saw his chance to start the two sides fighting again. Rodor! Rodor was important. If he could remove Rodor ... He could then go back to camp, and make up a story about how some Vikings had surprised them and taken Rodor prisoner. The King and his chiefs would be angry. They would be sure to attack the Vikings then.

Wulfgar and Rodor climbed down the ridge into the thick forest below. For Wulfgar, the moment had come. The moment to take Rodor.

If Rodor had turned to look at Wulfgar at that moment he would have seen a blood-chilling sight. He would have seen the colour drain from Wulfgar's face as a smothering darkness rose about him. He would have seen the Viran darkness in Wulfgar.

# Chapter 2

All Biff knew was that she was in thick, tangled undergrowth. She struggled free of branches and thorns and scrambled over a fallen tree.

A little way ahead, Chip had found a path. He was nursing a long scratch on his arm.

Suddenly there came the sound of squealing. A young boar burst through a mass of ferns and raced straight towards them.

In an instant, two arrows thwacked into the ground, just missing the boar's legs. Biff dived clear as the boar leapt past her. But Chip was caught directly in front of it. All he could do was turn and run as the terrified boar plunged on after him.

Biff started to run after Chip, but another arrow thumped into the path in front of her. She stood still, hardly daring to breathe.

The forest fell silent. Then, without a noise, a Viking boy stepped forward from the undergrowth. He held another arrow taut in his bow. It was pointed straight at Biff. She opened her mouth to speak.

"Sshh!" the boy hissed. "I've got you, you Saxon spy! Come with me!"

Biff had no choice. The boy kept his bow and arrow trained on her, and they headed back to the Viking camp.

Meanwhile, Chip continued to crash through the forest. As he ran, he turned to see if the boar was still behind him. But just then he stumbled over something solid, and fell heavily to the ground.

To Chip's amazement, a boy lay tied up at his feet. The boy opened his mouth to speak. "Rodo ... Wulf. Beware!" he managed to mutter. Chip was confused. A wolf? He nervously looked around – and found himself looking straight at the sharp end of a sword.

A Viking girl stood pointing the sword at Chip. From her shoulder hung several dead rabbits. "So!" she smiled. "We lost a boar, but caught a couple of Saxons."

The boar! Chip opened his mouth to speak. He wanted to ask about Biff, but the girl raised a finger to her lips.

"Sshh!" she said. "Saxon soldiers, everywhere!" She flicked her sword towards Chip and Rodor. "You must come with me," she muttered. "But do not make a sound!"

# Chapter 3

Meanwhile, back at the Saxon camp, Wulfgar had made up a story about how Rodor had been captured by Viking soldiers. The Saxon chiefs were furious. "War!" they all shouted.

Wulfgar smiled to himself as he listened to their angry reaction. If only they knew the truth! That in fact, he had used the power of his Viran stare to wipe Rodor's memory, and left him to the darkness of the forest.

Like a pack of barking dogs, the chiefs argued about what to do next. Only King Alfred sat as still as a statue, listening. In his hand he clutched a scroll. It was the peace treaty he had hoped to offer the Vikings. Suddenly he stood up and threw the peace treaty into the centre of the room.

"War?" he shouted. "Are we to throw away the chance of peace so easily?"

Chief Edwin, Rodor's father, stepped forward. "But they have my son!" he pleaded.

Alfred rested his hand on Edwin's shoulder. "And how will attacking them help that?" he asked.

Edwin lowered his head in sadness.

"No!" continued Alfred. "The time has come to talk. It is only by understanding that we can settle our differences!"

The King pointed to the treaty that lay at their feet. "It is the only way to end this hatred."

Wulfgar struggled to hide his Viran nature. The King's words of hope raised an angry darkness in him.

King Alfred turned to Wulfgar. For a moment, Wulfgar thought the King might be on to him. “Wulfgar!” Alfred said. “As you can speak so many languages, I should like you to go to the Vikings and read the peace treaty to them.”

The King looked around the room. "Are we agreed?"

The room fell silent. Then slowly, Chief Edwin picked up the treaty and handed it to Wulfgar. "We are agreed," he said.

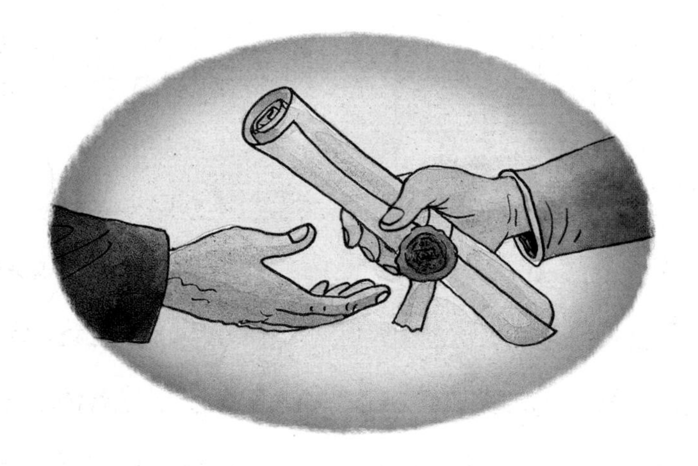

# Chapter 4

Biff's Link signal kept breaking up. Tyler sat in Control straining to hear her. The Link speaker hissed and whirred beneath her voice. "... Lost Chip ... Link. I ... caught by ... Viking boy ... I am in Viking camp ... am ... frightened!"

"OK, Biff. Stay calm," said Tyler. "I'll try and locate Chip. Oh, and Biff?" he added. "Don't worry about the Vikings. They're not as mean and scary as history says they are. Download to follow. Out!"

"Easy for you to say, Tyler," muttered Biff as she closed her Link. She looked around. She was shut in a long narrow building. Through gaps in the wooden walls, Biff could see a bit of the Viking camp, the outer wall, and some large wooden gates. A group of soldiers crouched, playing a game with pebbles in the dust. A woman was cooking over a fire and singing gently to herself. As Biff listened, she thought of Chip and she felt very alone.

# Chapter 5

"It's no good!" said a voice from the undergrowth. The voice made Chip jump. From a bank of thick ferns, the Viking girl – her name was Inga – suddenly appeared.

Chip and Rodor had been waiting while Inga checked to see if they could sneak back into the Viking camp, just beyond the trees where they hid. Now, she had returned, and she didn't look happy.

"Saxon soldiers!" she whispered. "We'll have to wait till it gets really dark. One good thing, though." Inga pulled some tree bark from her pocket. "I found this!"

"What is it?" asked Chip.

Inga glanced at Rodor who was still muttering to himself, as if he were in a dream. "Medicine," she said. She began to grind the bark into a pulp. "An old Viking remedy. It is good for the head."

Suddenly, Inga whirled round. A little way from where they were hiding stood a wild boar. Even Chip could see it was acting strangely. It stood still, sniffing the air, with every hair on its back bristling.

Just then, a horseman appeared. He was heading in the direction of the Viking camp, but also straight into the path of the snarling boar.

The boar stood its ground and waited, as if frozen to the spot.

At the very last moment, the boar sprung into life and charged. Just the sound of its snarl was enough.

The horse reared up in terror. The horseman was thrown heavily to the ground, his face twisted in fury.

Chip shuddered. He could see now why the boar had acted so strangely. It had sensed something strange. Something evil. It had sensed a Viran.

Wulfgar got to his feet and tried to grab hold of the terrified horse, but it shied away. He raised his arm in anger, and the horse turned and bolted.

Without stopping, even for a moment, Wulfgar began to walk. He didn't even look round. Had he done so, he would have seen King Alfred's peace treaty. It was lying on the forest floor where he had fallen from his horse.

# Chapter 6

Inga broke the seal on the scroll of paper and read. "The Saxon language is similar to ours. I can understand bits of this, but not much." She handed it to Chip to read, but he could only understand one word – "Alfred ..."

Suddenly Rodor stood up. "Let me read it!" he cried. "Alfred, King of Saxon England ..." He began to read, slowly at first but then with more confidence.

Rodor's mind was beginning to focus. Wulfgar's mind-stare was wearing off.

As Rodor read, his mind cleared and his memory began to return. "This is King Alfred's peace treaty! That was Wulfgar who ...?" Rodor stopped. At the name 'Wulfgar', he shuddered. His mind had flooded with terrible memories of what had happened to him. "It was Wulfgar. He did this to me. I don't know how he did it, but he wiped my mind."

"I think I know," said Chip as he reached for his Link. "We need to stop Wulfgar, and I need to find my sister!"

# Chapter 7

"So Chip's Link had turned itself off. He must have knocked it when the boar chased him." Tyler was talking to Biff on the Link. "Anyway, I've told him where you are. He's not far from you. He's with a Viking girl. They'll come and find you. But they've just seen the Viran in the forest. Chip thinks he might be coming to the Viking camp. They want to see what he's up to first. Tyler out."

No sooner had Biff closed her Link, than she heard a cry from a guard on the camp wall. “Stranger at the gates!”

In the moonlight, Biff could see the outline of Viking soldiers. With swords drawn they cautiously opened one of the gates. A figure stepped forward from the shadows. It was Wulfgar. He was about to spin more lies in his quest for chaos.

“What is it you want, stranger?” asked one of the soldiers.

“I bring news,” hissed Wulfgar. “The Saxons are sharpening their swords. They are preparing for war. Attack now, while you still have the chance.”

“Why should we believe you, stranger?” asked one of the Vikings.

“Then don’t!” sneered Wulfgar. “But can you really afford not to?”

"The Saxons believe you hold one of their sons," Wulfgar continued. "He goes by the name of Rodor."

"There is no one here with that name," answered one of the Vikings.

"Even if what you say is true," sneered Wulfgar, "the Saxons will never believe you. King Alfred is looking for a reason to fight."

Suddenly Biff heard a new voice. "You speak lies, Wulfgar!"

Wulfgar spun round as Rodor stepped out of the darkness behind him.

"The Saxons and the Vikings shall know the truth of what you have done," growled Rodor. Wulfgar looked confused for a moment. How had Rodor escaped? After all, he had tied him up and left him deep in the forest.

Wulfgar turned to the Vikings. "This boy has been sent to trick you," he barked.

"No!" shouted Rodor. "King Alfred wants to offer a peace treaty to you, Vikings!"

"Where is your proof?" laughed Wulfgar.

"Here!" Rodor raised his arm in the air. In his fist he clenched the peace treaty that Wulfgar had dropped.

Wulfgar felt for the scroll Alfred had given him, but it wasn't there. In a raging darkness, he charged at Rodor.

Rodor flinched in fear. But at that moment Chip stepped forward. His Zaptrap glinted in the moonlight. "The game's up, Viran," he said.

"Never!" screamed the Viran as he turned and fled into the night.

# Chapter 8

Chip tore through the dark forest. He couldn't see the Viran up ahead, but he could hear him.

He knew Rodor and Biff would be safe as long as the Saxons didn't attack. He hoped that Inga would show the Vikings the peace treaty.

But his fear was that the Viran might have another trick ready that would restart the fight between the two armies. If a battle started, what would happen to Biff? If only for her, the Viran had to be stopped.

Chip's legs began to feel heavy. He was breathing hard. He felt as if he were running uphill. He was. The Viran was heading up the ridge towards the beacon. He was going to light it. It would summon the Saxon army. Chip had to stop him at all costs.

At the top, the Viran stopped at the beacon. He was fumbling in his pocket. His face twisted into a terrifying snarl as he watched Chip hurl a Zaptrap towards him.

# Chapter 9

Inga had only just let Biff out when a mighty cry went up in the Viking camp. High on the ridge, a cone of flame lit the night sky. The Saxon beacon had been lit. Viking soldiers called to one another as they watched the Saxon army gathering. "Make ready! Make ready!" they cried.

Biff's Link whirred in her pocket. Tyler had sent a message from Chip.

DOWNLOAD FROM TYLER

Chip on ridge. Viran caught. Sparks from Zaptrap lit the beacon. It is up to you to stop the battle.

Biff's mind raced. How could she possibly stop a battle? She looked at Inga and Rodor. He stood clutching the peace treaty nervously. All around them, Viking soldiers were moving out of the camp, ready to fight.

Suddenly, Biff grabbed Rodor and Inga and ran as fast as she could toward the Saxon army.

From the ridge, Chip watched as the two armies gathered to face each other across an open field. Chip shook his head sadly. Though the Viran had been caught, he had won. The battle seemed impossible to avoid.

Then to his amazement, he saw Biff, Rodor and Inga running past the Viking

soldiers and across the field towards the Saxons.

On seeing Rodor running towards them, the Saxons started to cheer. King Alfred stepped forward to greet him. Many of the Saxon chiefs gathered round Rodor, Biff and Inga.

With his army following behind him, King Alfred started to walk towards the Vikings.

Biff held her breath as she waited for the moment the two armies would meet. With every soldier holding a weapon at the ready, she felt sure that a terrible battle was about to begin.

A few paces away from the Vikings, King Alfred stopped. The Vikings tensed as the King drew his sword. Then, slowly, he sank its blade into the muddy ground at his feet.

"Vikings. We could fight over these lands forever. But why, when there is enough soil for all to plough and grow their crops?" Alfred stepped forward and held out his hands. "Let us agree to divide this island between us and live side by side in peace.

You rule by your laws, and we Saxons by ours. Our laws and our languages are so similar that, in time, we could even trade with one another."

Slowly, one after another, the Vikings pushed their swords into the earth.

No longer invaders, the Vikings were here to stay.

Biff opened her Link. "Time to go," she said.

# Glossary

**bolted** *(page 26)* Ran off. *He raised his arm in anger, and the horse turned and bolted.*

**clenched** *(page 32)* Grasped tightly. *In his fist he clenched the peace treaty that Wulfgar had dropped.*

**peace treaty** *(page 15)* A formal agreement to make peace between two sides that have been at war. *It was the peace treaty he had hoped to offer the Vikings.*

**shied** *(page 26)* When horses shy, they panic and kick out with their front legs. *Wulfgar got to his feet and tried to grab hold of the terrified horse, but it shied away.*

**smothering** *(page 8)* Covering something thickly or in a way that makes you choke. *He would have seen the colour drain from Wulfgar's face as a smothering darkness rose about him.*

**surrendering** *(page 4)* Giving in, or agreeing to let the enemy win in a battle. *They were close to surrendering.*

**undergrowth** *(page 10)* Bushes and other plants that grow under trees. *... a Viking boy stepped forward from the undergrowth.*

**Thesaurus: Another word for ...**

**clenched** *(page 32)* seized, gripped, grasped.

# Tyler's Mission Report

| Location: | Date: |
| --- | --- |
| Wessex, England. | 878 |
| Mission Status: | Viran Status: |
| Successful. | 1 zaptrapped. |

Notes: Viking Invaders? Saxon settlers? Here's a thought.

Wherever you look in history, the people at that time are influenced by loads of stuff that is new and from other countries. We tend to think that countries, and the people who live there, stay the same. But in fact countries are always changing: accepting new people and new ideas. Soon, what was once 'different' becomes part of what is 'normal'. It becomes part of what a nation is. Then at some point, new people come along and things change all over again.

Take me, for example. I'm half French. I reckon if we all looked back far enough we'd find our ancestors come from somewhere else other than where we are today. We are all invaders and we are all settlers.

Sign off: ............Tyler............................

# History: downloaded!

## Vikings and Saxons

The Saxons came to expect the terrifying Viking raids from across the North Sea. Everyone knew what the Vikings wanted – treasure. The Saxons did their best to hide it, whilst the Vikings tore village after village apart to find it.

*But by the 9th Century things began to change. The Vikings were not after treasure so much as land. They wanted to settle.*

By the 870s, Northumbria, East Anglia and Mercia were all under Viking influence. Now the Vikings turned their attention to the last great Saxon Kingdom, Wessex – and its king, Alfred.

Wessex very nearly fell to the Vikings. Had it done so, history would have taken a very different course. But against all odds, Alfred and his part-time army managed to defeat the Vikings and gain peace.

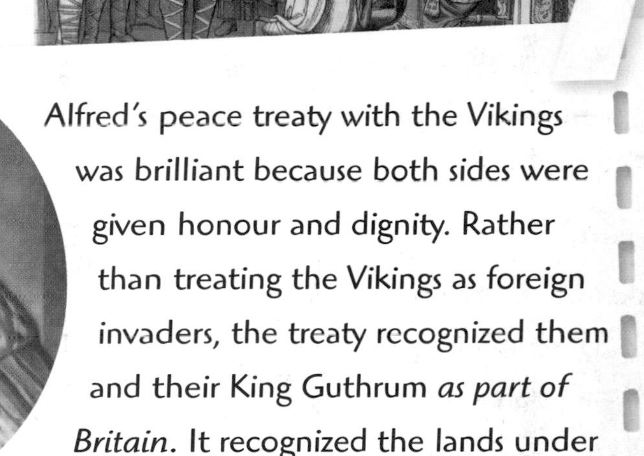

The Viking king, Guthrum, makes peace with the Saxons.

King Alfred

Alfred's peace treaty with the Vikings was brilliant because both sides were given honour and dignity. Rather than treating the Vikings as foreign invaders, the treaty recognized them and their King Guthrum *as part of Britain*. It recognized the lands under Viking rule, known as Danelaw, and agreed laws to help the Saxons and the Vikings to live as neighbours.

For more information, see the Time Chronicles website:
**www.oxfordprimary.co.uk/timechronicles**

# A voice from history

When the Vikings came they hit us fast and hard. They hit us when we least expected it ... Christmas. Caked in freezing mud and forever hungry, we spent that winter hiding in a marsh. In those dark days, we often wondered if it was all worth it. I mean, what were we fighting for? A few scattered homesteads, and a handful of animals? Was that all we were? Was that all we stood for?

In a strange kind of way, the Vikings did us a favour. They made us ask these questions of ourselves. And so, with our victory, we decided to rebuild our kingdom. I'm not just talking about building a proper army and navy, or fortifying our towns. All this we did. No, I'm talking about building a culture. Our history, written down in poems and songs. And books, the best we could find, translated into our language. Now *that* is worth fighting for.